Lady of Hope

Lady of Hope

A Poetry Collection

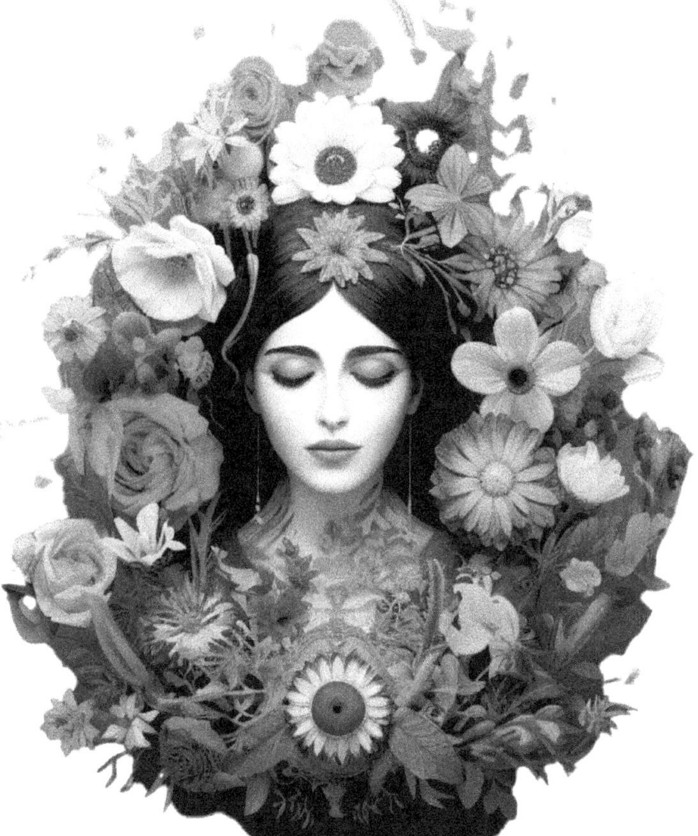

King Bean

allwrite publishing
Atlanta, GA

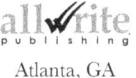

Lady of Hope: A Poetry Collection
Copyright 2024

All rights reserved.

No part of this book may be reproduced or transmitted in any form or by any means, electronic or mechanical, including photocopying, recording or by any information storage and retrieval system, without written permission from the author, except for the inclusion of brief quotations in a review.

ISBN: 978-1-941716-15-1 (print)
ISBN: 978-1-941716-19-9 (ebook)

Library of Congress Control Number: 2024901854

Edited by Annette R. Johnson

Printed in the United States of America

Dedication

I would like to dedicate this book to the love of my life, my husband Martin E. Bean, for whom he caresses my soul every day with softness and tenderness.

Table of Contents

Preface, ix

The Official Language 11

Endless Soul 13

Lulu 15

Close Lovers 17

Don't Say It 19

Othello 21

For Us 23

Lost Walker 25

Opium Encounters 27

What Love Left 29

But Love Is Over 31

Love 33

American Holocaust 35

Sorrow 37

Virginity 39

Enslaved Soul 41

Spiderwebs 43

Feelings 45

Ostracism 47

Road to Freedom 49

About the Author 49

Preface

When you turn this page, sit comfortably and relax. Hopefully, it will be on a sunny afternoon while you're overlooking the sea, either alone or with that person who wants to caress your soul. If you choose a rainy afternoon, make sure someone is strumming beautiful guitar chords in a hectic, crazy gathering.

Many of my readers have been left with a bitter taste in their mouths from the wait and what happened after, wanting to know: "What did the lovers do?" and "What was the end of Esperanza?" and "Do Arab women really exist?"

I leave you the promise of a second meeting, in which I will reveal many ghosts that want to be seen and appreciated. Meanwhile, let us shout in unison: *Long live poetry, an inexhaustible force of love and faith!*

The book includes a link to the audio version of each poem, so enjoy it any way you like!

The Official Language

The little white children lay down in the sand,
Their blonde hair radiated tenderness.
On the path to school,
The little Latin children danced Macarena,
Their scruffy backpacks contained bread and fruit.
On the path to school,
The little black children talked about adventures
Their tireless legs ran across the clear plains.
On the path to school,
The little Chinese children multiplied mentally,
Their sharp minds envisioned the blue horizon.
On the path to school,
The little children rested, danced, spoke, learned,
So tender, so hungry, so eager, so inquisitive
They talked differently but understood each other
Because they spoke only one language.

To LISTEN to the poem being read by the author, SCAN the QR code (above) using the built-in camera app on your cell phone or tablet. Point the camera at the QR code. Tap the banner that appears on your phone or tablet. Follow the instructions on the screen to access the audio file.

Endless Soul

The rain comes and soaks the soul,
such that my eyes cannot see into the misty distance.

Still everything is clear and wonderful,
causing me to imagine him in front of me as I recline at his feet.

Rainwater and tears bathe my hair and body,
having no worse lover than one who can't weather a storm.

Even when he lies inert and pale,
don't let the dream end, please let it never end.

Let me taste his soul once again,
drinking the most bitter coffee, filled with uncertainty and fear.

The soul roams every corner of the world,
looking for someone that claims its endless existence.

To LISTEN to the poem being read by the author, SCAN the QR code (above) using the built-in camera app on your cell phone or tablet. Point the camera at the QR code. Tap the banner that appears on your phone or tablet. Follow the instructions on the screen to access the audio file.

Lulu

Lulu walks down the avenue.
She faces the raging wind.
Lulu pulls up her crinoline.
She fixes her flowing dress.
Lulu walks to the corner shop,
She meets her fiancé there.
Lulu pulls up his pant leg.
She exposes his chicken legs.
The groom looks scared.
He looks at her legs and says:
"Oh my, Lulu, for God's sake!
How ugly, how ugly your shins are."

To LISTEN to the poem being read by the author, SCAN the QR code (above) using the built-in camera app on your cell phone or tablet. Point the camera at the QR code. Tap the banner that appears on your phone or tablet. Follow the instructions on the screen to access the audio file.

Close Lovers

On a warm night
Two lovers spoke
Happily they shared
Close to his bedroom

She plucked roses
He kissed her feet
She toasted with wine
Close to his heart

To LISTEN to the poem being read by the author, SCAN the QR code (above) using the built-in camera app on your cell phone or tablet. Point the camera at the QR code. Tap the banner that appears on your phone or tablet. Follow the instructions on the screen to access the audio file.

Don't Say It

Don't say what you don't know.
If you don't know, don't invent it.
They will call you a liar!

Don't say what you didn't hear.
If you don't hear it firsthand, don't repeat it
They'll figure out what you don't know.

Don't say bad things about a stranger.
The person you don't know could help you.
They could introduce you to great people.

Don't say yes for no.
When you say no, you become a lady.
You'll be desired, like forbidden fruit.

Don't say no just for the sake of it.
When you say yes, you must commit.
Life changes as you respond.

To LISTEN to the poem being read by the author, SCAN the QR code (above) using the built-in camera app on your cell phone or tablet. Point the camera at the QR code. Tap the banner that appears on your phone or tablet. Follow the instructions on the screen to access the audio file.

Othello

His tar eyes devoured her.
His star apple mouth kissed her.
His luminous teeth bit her.
Her woolen hair caressed his frame.

She asked, "Who are you?"
He said, "I am Othello, the Merciless!"
"What makes you fall in love, Othello?"
"You are the best, most ardent lover!"

To LISTEN to the poem being read by the author, SCAN the QR code (above) using the built-in camera app on your cell phone or tablet. Point the camera at the QR code. Tap the banner that appears on your phone or tablet. Follow the instructions on the screen to access the audio file.

For Us

Music, lights, hubbub
The fantasy begins
Long live the Guaro
Long live the women
The males of Michoacan are the bravest
Raise your glass and toast the females
from Morelia, who are the coolest ones
Come on my love, go ahead
Raise your Tecate and toast us
For the males of Michoacan are the bravest

To LISTEN to the poem being read by the author, SCAN the QR code (above) using the built-in camera app on your cell phone or tablet. Point the camera at the QR code. Tap the banner that appears on your phone or tablet. Follow the instructions on the screen to access the audio file.

Lost Walker

Silence, sadness and death
Darkness seeks shelter in my ribs
Skies tormented with signs of a storm
You throw your hope to the wind
Useless is your search for new paths
Look at your own land
Look how he bleeds out
Look, he's no longer alive
He can't take it anymore

To LISTEN to the poem being read by the author, SCAN the QR code (above) using the built-in camera app on your cell phone or tablet. Point the camera at the QR code. Tap the banner that appears on your phone or tablet. Follow the instructions on the screen to access the audio file.

Opium Encounters

I am better than you, for I am African.
I am both a target of marvel and hatred that expands across the globe.
I am dark as onyx and strong as steel.
My blood is an ocean of fierce passion and soul.
They secretly envy the way the earth vibrates when I walk.

I am better than you, for I am European.
I am who everyone says yes to and whose women they prefer.
I am always trying to lead at any cost.
My skin is as snowy white as my hair at times.
They look to me for progress and prosperity.

I am better than you, for I am Hispanic.
I am a mixture of a thousand men, the faith of a thousand cultures.
I am fruit, the torture, and passion of the Earth.
My life is arduous, being familiar poverty and ruin.
They know my potential and love of God.

I am better than everyone, for I am Asian.
I am the gray matter, indestructible because my intelligence is superior.
I am resourceful, benefiting from the soil and sea.
My eyes catch and scrutinize everything.
They study my ways to improve their lives.

Woman, at last, your color doesn't matter!
Your hemisphere of origin doesn't matter!
"For dust you are and to dust you will return."

To LISTEN to the poem being
read by the author, SCAN the
QR code (above) using the built-
in camera app on your cell phone
or tablet. Point the camera at the
QR code. Tap the banner that
appears on your phone or tablet.
Follow the instructions on the
screen to access the audio file.

What Love Left

In the depths of my body wonders emerged.
The future of the world left its footprint.
Your departure will not erase it.
My forgetfulness remains.
No escape offered.
Beautiful she is.
Like no other.
Love within.
Mother.

To LISTEN to the poem being read by the author, SCAN the QR code (above) using the built-in camera app on your cell phone or tablet. Point the camera at the QR code. Tap the banner that appears on your phone or tablet. Follow the instructions on the screen to access the audio file.

But Love Is Over

And I tie myself to her black hair, stroking it sweetly and slowly
And I drink from her sweetest lips, the most delicious honey
And I taste the juiciest fruits, between moans and lamentations
And I sink into her belly like a woodpecker, piercing fresh wood

And we dance the brilliant samba
And we enjoy the fiery carnival
But love is over now
See you tomorrow

To LISTEN to the poem being read by the author, SCAN the QR code (above) using the built-in camera app on your cell phone or tablet. Point the camera at the QR code. Tap the banner that appears on your phone or tablet. Follow the instructions on the screen to access the audio file.

Love

I want to tell you an unforgettable word: Love
And you will consider it the same way
But you won't feel it the way I feel it

The most perfect statement
And the best pronounced word
But on your lips, it will always be a mystery

To LISTEN to the poem being read by the author, SCAN the QR code (above) using the built-in camera app on your cell phone or tablet. Point the camera at the QR code. Tap the banner that appears on your phone or tablet. Follow the instructions on the screen to access the audio file.

American Holocaust

There was no next day, no second chances.
It arrived like a thief in the middle of the night.
It took over all minds and bodies as it seeped.
Those who were awake were covered in black soot.
They no longer saw anything except their own end.
The white of their eyes and teeth were hints of remains.
Life, liberty and love combusted with the cloud of death.
The lethal gas killed everything, including insects and vermin.
The roar on the continent made the rest of the world vibrate.
The other continents reported the news the next day.
The third part of America was gone, nothing remained.

To LISTEN to the poem being read by the author, SCAN the QR code (above) using the built-in camera app on your cell phone or tablet. Point the camera at the QR code. Tap the banner that appears on your phone or tablet. Follow the instructions on the screen to access the audio file.

Sorrow

What happened to Esperanza?
They say she became old and ugly.
What happened to her true love?
He ate too much and his face swelled.
His flesh hangs off his bloated body.
He looks like an old sausage.
So, everyone wonders about her.
What happened to Esperanza?
Is she still the prettiest?
The poor thing carries a pain in her soul.
Who can handle her sorrow?
Where is her true love?
He went to Thailand.

To LISTEN to the poem being read by the author, SCAN the QR code (above) using the built-in camera app on your cell phone or tablet. Point the camera at the QR code. Tap the banner that appears on your phone or tablet. Follow the instructions on the screen to access the audio file.

Virginity

You emerged like chains that trapped my existence.
You created an abyss of pain unleashed over time.
You left me with the absence of decency and desire.
In our sky, dark clouds will always appear.
They cover the sun, never illuminating our future.
What did you do with my life, my dreams?
Why did you lie and laugh at me?
How can you even be human?
My purity was transformed to an orgy.
You took disrespect to the maximum.
You played with me like a newborn child.
You deposited so much filth.
All this from a macho boy,
Who never knew true love.
You did me a great favor,
You took a big weight off me.
You showed me impure love.

To LISTEN to the poem being read by the author, SCAN the QR code (above) using the built-in camera app on your cell phone or tablet. Point the camera at the QR code. Tap the banner that appears on your phone or tablet. Follow the instructions on the screen to access the audio file.

Enslaved Soul

Impenetrable armor
Black, shiny leather
Rhythmic march
Bedazzled heart
Honeysuckle eyes
Golden glowing skin
Kissed by the sun's rays
Bright, white smile
Shackled feet and hands

Persecuted slave,
What is your story?
What is in your soul?
What is in your heart?
I want to get closer to you.
Give me your hand.

To LISTEN to the poem being read by the author, SCAN the QR code (above) using the built-in camera app on your cell phone or tablet. Point the camera at the QR code. Tap the banner that appears on your phone or tablet. Follow the instructions on the screen to access the audio file.

Spiderwebs

Cobwebs cover my face and body.
I feel as old and tired as I may look.
I'm rowing down the stream of years.
I won't know when to stop.
For the rudder is not mine.
The Lord God guides the helm.
I want to be on board for many years.
I want to see you become a mother.
I want to feel your joy and love.

To LISTEN to the poem being read by the author, SCAN the QR code (above) using the built-in camera app on your cell phone or tablet. Point the camera at the QR code. Tap the banner that appears on your phone or tablet. Follow the instructions on the screen to access the audio file.

Feelings

Resentment. Selfishness. Falsehood.
Not even crying can wash away the deepest grief.
Not even fire can destroy the cruelest memories.
Not even time can diminish the worst betrayals.
I hate the power of negative feelings.
The pain can be so intense, not giving way to hope.
The heart remains broken and grieving for relief.
What lives in your broken heart?
Why don't you give way to light?
How do you live with this impasse?
Move it away. Declare it away. Pray it away.
You will be reborn in another space.
On this route, it will find you.
Head toward your resting position.
This was your original position.

To LISTEN to the poem being read by the author, SCAN the QR code (above) using the built-in camera app on your cell phone or tablet. Point the camera at the QR code. Tap the banner that appears on your phone or tablet. Follow the instructions on the screen to access the audio file.

Ostracism

Years in solitude and misunderstood
A love who once lived with hope
The flight of a million eagles await
Only one resists the game
Locked in the labyrinth of her exile
She is left behind and caged
Trapped in the black tower of memories
PUM PUM PAM PAM
The drum rings in harmony
PUM PUM PAM PAM
The heart responds
PUM PUM PAM PAM
Let the joy begin

To LISTEN to the poem being read by the author, SCAN the QR code (above) using the built-in camera app on your cell phone or tablet. Point the camera at the QR code. Tap the banner that appears on your phone or tablet. Follow the instructions on the screen to access the audio file.

Road to Freedom

I seek to recover the lost faith tied to your corruption and capture.
I will silently climb the infinite because a great future awaits.
There is neither a song nor a drumbeat in the thicket to lead us.
I only have my feverish breath, intoxicating the eerie blackness.
Maybe someone is waiting for us, to take us to another world.
As intercontinental orphans, we continue running blindly.
Sleepwalkers, we are fatigued but encouraged by freedom.
Fear behind and ahead, we could fall charmingly into lethargy.
Eyes lifted, hearts divided between agony and aspirations.
On the road to freedom, we have but one combined sentiment:
Hope of what was dreamed of and deep fear of achieving it.

To LISTEN to the poem being read by the author, SCAN the QR code (above) using the built-in camera app on your cell phone or tablet. Point the camera at the QR code. Tap the banner that appears on your phone or tablet. Follow the instructions on the screen to access the audio file.

About the Author

A native of Panama, Maureen King Bean has lived in the United States since 1984, first in Lilburn, GA, and later in Kendall, FL, where she lives with her husband, Martin E. Bean. Maureen first graduated as a Spanish Philology major from U.A.C.A in Costa Rica and later as Master in Spanish Culture and Literature from University of Salamanca. She taught Spanish in elementary school for more than 20 years in Miami Dade Public Schools, Atlanta Public Schools, and Bartow County Schools. Maureen is currently working for Miami Dade College as an ESOL instructor. Meanwhile, she continues celebrating life and is grateful for the creative gifts and opportunities God has given her.

www.ingramcontent.com/pod-product-compliance
Lightning Source LLC
Chambersburg PA
CBHW050046080526
44586CB00014B/1480